Fireworks

Managing anger in young children

by
Dr Hannah Mortimer

Acknowledgement

With acknowledgements and thanks to the families I work with who have tried out these approaches and managed to stay calm with each other in the process!

A QEd Publication

Published in 2007

© Hannah Mortimer

ISBN 978 1 898873 16 7

All rights reserved. Permission is given to the purchaser only to copy pages 13, 16, 19, 20, 21, 22, 27, 31, 33, 34, 36, 37, 40, 42 and 43. No further part of this publication may be reproduced, stored in a retrieval system, or transmitted in any form or by any means, electronic, mechanical, photocopying, recording or otherwise, without the prior written permission of the publisher.

The right of Hannah Mortimer to be identified as Author of this work has been asserted by her in accordance with the Copyright, Designs and Patents Act 1988.

British Library Cataloguing
A catalogue record for this book is available from the British Library.

Published by QEd Publications, 39 Weeping Cross, Stafford ST17 0DG
Tel: 01785 620364
Fax: 01785 607797
Web site: www.qed.uk.com
Email: orders@qed.uk.com

Printed by Gutenberg Press, Malta.

Contents

	Page
Introduction	4
Who the book is for	4
Why was this book written?	4
'Talk through' approaches	5
What do we know about emotions?	5
Anger management	6
The firework model	6
How to use this book	7
Chapter 1 – Getting started	8
Involve the child	8
Who is the best person to help?	9
A shopping list	9
A quiet corner	10
Planning your sessions	10
Ages and stages	10
Chapter 2 – Twelve practical sessions	11
Session 1 – Making a work box	12
Session 2 – All about me	13
Session 3 – My fireworks	18
Session 4 – All about fuses	21
Session 5 – Spotting a trigger	23
Session 6 – Acting it out	25
Session 7 & 8 – Relax!	26
Session 9 – Speaking out	31
Session 10 – Thinking positively	35
Session 11 – Making a plan	38
Session 12 – How did I do?	41
References, useful books and resources	44

Introduction

Who the book is for

This book is part of a series written to help adults provide emotional support to young children aged 5 to 11. Sometimes aspects of their social and emotional development which are underdeveloped get in the way of their happiness or well-being and need working on. This book focuses on anger management. The other book in this series is *Worry Box: Managing anxiety in young children* (Mortimer, 2007). The books are written in an accessible and practical style so that a parent, carer, support assistant, childminder or mentor can work out the most suitable approach for the individual child concerned and 'pick and mix' activities and talking points to fill a number of sessions.

Why was this book written?

These books were written to fill a perceived need. In the author's experience, there are several very useful books available for supporting older primary and secondary age children in groups (some of these are listed on page 43) but fewer available for individual children aged five to eleven. The author found herself adapting material to suit these younger children and also writing individual packages so that parents or professionals could support the children they were working with. The children themselves came with a variety of needs:

- Some had been referred to a child psychologist or behaviour support teacher because of a recognised difficulty in emotional and social development – a very short 'fuse' or a high level of anxiety.
- A few parents or carers recognised that their child was being significantly affected by a major change in their life (such as a bereavement or a family breakdown) and were asking for advice on what they could do to support their child and to minimise any negative emotional effects.
- In some cases, teachers and parents had identified a child as having additional or different needs on account of a social and emotional difficulty and a piece of work had been identified at a special educational needs (SEN) review meeting, such as 'anger management' or 'stress counselling'.
- In other cases, parents simply saw that a short temper, anxiety or inability to make friends was getting in the way of their child's happiness or well-being. They wanted a discreet and family-centred approach for helping their child to cope better.

We know from research on supporting individuals after major traumas that the best people to help and support them are usually those nearest and dearest. Only if we become 'stuck' in dealing with our grief, anxiety or anger do we need more specialist help. In the same way, the author found that when she gave families 'a job to do' in order to tackle their child's emotional difficulties, families usually found the work they did together helpful and supportive and family relationships grew closer in the process. Without a practical framework it is difficult to 'get started' and a book such as this can act as a starting point for more open communication and more sharing of feelings within the family.

Of course, if you try this approach and the child is just as angry at the end of the course, you should not hesitate in seeking further professional support. You should also stop the course and seek advice if the child is becoming far more angry than before. If the child has been following the approach at school, then a referral from the SEN co-ordinator to a behaviour support teacher might be an option. If you are working together at home, then you might ask your GP to consider a referral to the Child and Adult Mental Health Services (CAMHS).

'Talk through' approaches

The books use a 'talk through' approach to provide a framework for the adult and child to talk and work together. You might have met this approach before in the book *Taking Part* (Mortimer, 2000) which allows adults to talk through the statutory assessment of SEN with a child. These frameworks should not be followed verbatim and should be used flexibly so that each piece of work seems to flow naturally and feel appropriate for your situation. You are encouraged to think creatively as you work together with the child and to adapt or even design your own sessions as they develop. Though written as an interaction between an adult and child, it is up to the adult to phrase the wording and adapt it to suit the situation, age and stage of the child.

What do we know about emotions?

We know that anger is chemically based and controlled by a complex and finely balanced system within the brain and the nervous system. We know that it forms part of an important mechanism for affecting our behaviour and originates in the 'fight or flight' mechanism we needed for survival as cave dwellers. It was important for us to have a rapid mechanism that allowed us to see a beast and make split second decisions to either chase and attack it or to flee for our lives. It was no good pausing to think about it. This is why the emotional part of our brain is sometimes called the 'primitive' area of the brain – it acts without logical thought and almost despite ourselves.

We may have evolved and developed much higher thinking skills, but our emotional brains continue to be vitally important for learning which things in life to avoid and which to approach and explore. Very young children are inevitably driven more by their emotional brains than their logic – they are 'all needs and reactions'. However, in time, toddlers and pre-school children develop the language and understanding to link their emotional feelings to their words and their experiences and thereby to develop 'emotional literacy'.

The fact is that our emotional brains can switch in without our being fully aware of why or where the feelings are coming from. Some people talk about this phenomenon as forming part of our 'emotional intelligence' – if we can understand where our feelings are coming from and what emotional experiences or 'baggage' have formed them, then we are emotionally intelligent individuals. For many of us, the picture is more complex and we have work to do on developing our 'emotional literacy' if we are to be better able to handle our emotions.

That, in a nutshell, is what this series is about – helping even young children to develop their emotional intelligence when it seems that their emotional brains continue to shout louder than their logical brains. Some children find it hard to integrate their emotions with their experiences and they remain very emotional individuals who *react* rather than *consider*.

Anger management

Anger management has two main components – managing the angry feelings and reactions, but also addressing the source of the anger. When planning how to support very angry children, the adults in their lives may need to find out where the strong feelings are coming from and do what can be done in order to address the root causes. Sometimes this will involve family work on relationships within the family, addressing any history of trauma and emotional damage, any deep seated phobias and any ongoing fears and stresses. This book does not cover that kind of specialist work. At another level, the child can be helped to deal with the emotional reactions that occur, understand where the feelings are coming from, challenge some of the thinking it seems to rouse in them and thereby learn to control their reactions. That is how this book can help.

The book is based loosely on cognitive behaviour therapy in which the child is helped to think about his/her feelings in a different way and thereby to feel more in control of them. You will also find some of the ideas from an approach called 'solution focused therapy'. These approaches are not magic wands and should never be used as a sticking plaster for serious emotional problems – 'fixing' a behaviour cannot also address an underlying emotional difficulty. That is why the approach is sometimes used as part of a wider menu of support with the aid of an outside professional. Nevertheless, if an emotional behaviour is getting in the way of a child's progress and happiness and if the child recognises this and wants to do some work on it, then it is well worth while trying the approach in this book within a home or educational setting.

The firework model

Losing your temper is a little like setting off a firework. There is usually a trigger that lights the fuse. Sometimes the fuse is long and it takes quite a time for the spark to reach the firework. Once it does – whoosh – the whole firework shoots off and there is simply no stopping it. If only we had spotted the trigger or dampened the spark when it was still burning slowly, we could have prevented it. But taking action when the firework has already 'blown' is simply too late and too dangerous. It can be difficult to put out a burning fuse in young children and the easiest way is to keep your own voice and attitude calm, relaxing and reassuring. At the very point when every muscle and nerve in our own bodies is telling us to raise our voices and get cross, the actual approach is the very opposite. This approach will help you as an adult to understand and make use of that fact.

How to use this book

Chapter One helps you to get started. You need to think about who will do the work and how to involve and engage the child fully in what you are doing. Chapter Two suggests twelve sessions that can be used flexibly and adapted to suit your situation, whether working at home with your own child or in an educational or out-of-school setting. At the end of the book is a resources section with helpful books and other resources. Throughout the book you will find activity sheets and questionnaires to enlarge and photocopy or give you ideas for drawing your own versions. These are for the child to complete with your help and to stick into their work file or scrapbook. There are also some comments from adults who have used or adapted the approach with children they have worked with.

Chapter 1

Getting Started

Involve the child

First of all you need to identify that there is a problem. There is no point embarking on this work if the child sees no need or does not understand what it is about. Something brought you to the point where you obtained this book and considered doing some work with the child. Put this into words and write it down for yourself. For example: 'Richard is fine until he does not get his own way. As soon as he feels thwarted, he loses his temper and as soon as he loses his temper, there's no way of negotiating with him – his temper is horrible for all of us.'

So far, you have *your* reasons for working together but they might not be Richard's. Look at what you have written and you might find one or two statements that are concrete, indisputable and clearly a problem for Richard. For example: 'Your temper is always getting you into trouble. People don't see your good side because of it. When you lose your temper, you can't think clearly and you're not in control. The trouble is, I lose mine too and then everything gets worse. Shall we do some work together on controlling our tempers?'

By now, Richard's parents or carers might also realise that there are other ways in which they can address the problem by looking at the underlying cause. If they are matching temper with temper, then they will be fanning the flames and making the situation far worse. If there is a lot of anger and shouting within the family, then perhaps Richard's temper is acting a little like a safety valve that signals 'enough!' In this case, he is only mirroring what the adults in his life do frequently and he has learned that when you really need something to happen, what you do is 'blow a fuse'. Perhaps what is needed is a much calmer way for his parents or carers to manage his behaviour. To help with this, QEd Publications have a series on managing difficult behaviour in calm and positive ways – *Managing your 4 to 8 year-old*; *Managing your 8 to 12 year-old*; and *Managing your 13 to 16 year-old*.

Remember that for some children the plan of action might have two levels – working on the underlying cause and managing the emotional reaction to it. Perhaps Richard is so angry because he is emotionally upset by a major change in his life (such as bereavement or family separation), because he is feeling horrible (as in a chronic medical conditions or illness), because he is stressed or traumatised about something (there may be problems at school such as bullying) or because his self-esteem is very low. If any of these are suspected, then Richard also needs help to address the underlying issues.

For example, you might try building in some work using a life storybook. A life storybook is just that – a scrapbook put together by an adult and child describing the child's life, family members, homes and major events or life changes. Photographs and the child's drawings are used to illustrate the story. The life storybook then becomes a useful prop for fetching out and talking about whenever child or carer need an excuse to talk about personal events and feelings. Failing that, as mentioned in the introduction, outside professional help through school or GP might be your best way forward.

Who is the best person to help?

If you are following the approach at home and there are two of you, talk to the child about who they would like to do their work with. Do not be upset if your child chooses the other parent if there are two of you – usually each parent is good for meeting different needs in their child. Whichever of you is chosen, make this an absolute priority and keep regular, protected time for it. Make sure you also have enough time to clear your own mind and become calm and receptive before you begin. You need to be aware, however, that sometimes children prefer to work with someone outside the immediate family.

If the approach is being used in school or another setting, then decide who will be regularly available for the child and who the child already feels close to and can trust. This might be a personal support assistant or a teacher who has been released by a classroom support assistant. Some schools might have carefully selected and screened volunteer mentors or parent helpers. This kind of work is also possible to do in out-of-school settings where there is a small amount of training and ongoing support from, for example, a Children's Centre team. Family support workers might be well placed for this work and these kinds of approaches are also used by community nurses or occupational therapists in Child and Adult Mental Health Services (CAMHS). The work should always have the full support and involvement of parents or carers.

A shopping list

You will need:
- an A4 box file, preferably new, 'cool' and one the child has chosen;
- a pack of brand new felt-tip pens in many colours;
- a craft box with scissors, glue stick, hole punch, thicker felt-tips etc.;
- a scrap book, A4 file pad or stack of A4 paper;
- party balloons for Session 7.

Put everything in the box file and keep it all safe and out of circulation between sessions.

A quiet corner

You also need to decide on a quiet place to be together for about 45 minutes each time for about ten to twelve sessions. Because the whole course will take several sessions, it is best to find a slot in your week when you both know you can be together on your own – plan it rather like a music lesson. You might decide to work once a week. You might enjoy it so much that you choose twice a week. Don't rush it any faster than that because it needs time to 'cook' in the child's head between sessions!

Planning your sessions

Read the whole book first so that you, the adult, know broadly what you will be doing together. Plan the first two or three sessions carefully, but then let the course take its own direction as your work together proceeds. Keep the content of future sessions secret from the child so that each session comes as a good surprise. Explain to the child that a lot of the work you will do is for fun, but it also has its serious side. By the end of the anger course, you will both have learned lots about how your tempers work and how they can be kept under control! Some of the sessions overlap with other books in this series. The overlap is intentional – first so that you can feel familiarity with the approach and second because certain units are useful for tackling different emotions, such as both worry and anger.

Ages and stages

Though the text tells the child to 'read' or 'write' something, you should adapt how you do the activities depending on the age and stage of the child. Younger children will need you to do all the reading and writing but even five year-olds can tell you what they want you to write for them or may want to copy pieces into their scrapbook if you help. Do not feel that you have to finish each session at one sitting. Once again, remain flexible and allow each to run into the next as you find some take longer or less time than others. Above all, 'go with the child' so that you are both really engaging with and thinking about your work together.

> *I wanted to use this approach because of his dreadful temper. I felt so confused by his anger and usually very guilty too. Sometimes I felt he was acting as a spoilt child and I'd be really strict and send him to his room where he'd just wreck it or come out again. Sometimes I felt it was because he had no confidence and I would tend to give in to him – just for peace, you know. So I was all over the place with him and so was he with me. I thought I knew where it was all coming from – I'd had a very angry break-up with his Dad but that was years ago. But for him it was all still there – the anger that is. So, with a bit of help from my health visitor, I decided to do two things. I'd be more consistent in managing his behaviour – not giving in, praising him a lot and sticking to what I said more. We'd also plan some times together to enjoy ourselves and help us both deal with things a bit more calmly – that's where the anger course came in use.*
>
> Mother of Adam, aged 8

Chapter 2

Twelve practical sessions

These sessions are written as an interaction between an adult and child. This avoids specifying gender and also makes the text seem more personal and directly relevant. For very young children, you will need to do all the reading, of course, and adapt the words to suit a younger age. For all children, you need to interpret the text flexibly and alter the style to suit your situation. The words simply give you both a starting point for the work you are doing together.

The sessions are numbered, but should not be followed blindly. After the first three sessions, adjust and develop as the child and the situation begin to lead you. The very first session is deliberately more impersonal than the rest to give you both time to settle in.

If you are working as a professional, make it clear that your work is normally confidential. You will agree with the child what can be shared with other adults in their life and what cannot. The only times when you would need to break confidentiality is if you have concerns about the child's safety or about breaking the law. Safeguarding children procedures are paramount over everything else you do in this course.

Session 1: Making a work box

Hello . . . . . Well done – you have decided to do some work on your temper to help you stay calmer, stay out of trouble and help you think more clearly. I hope you really enjoy the course and that it is useful. Take a moment to ask any questions or share any worries you have about the course now if you like.

Your first job is to prepare your work box. This is, in fact, your new box file. Decorate a large label and stick it onto the front – it should say 'WORK BOX – STRICTLY SECRET' and have your name on in large decorated letters. You won't need me for all of this session, but we'll make sure we can be together alone some of the time so that you can share it with me and I can admire it.

Well done . . . . . that's the end of your first session! Give the work box to me so I can keep it somewhere safe.

Notes for adults

Keep this work personal by using the child's name frequently. Try to let the child work as independently as possible on their work box so that they feel proud of what they have done and personally involved with the work you will be doing together. Use this session to settle in together and keep it relaxed and encouraging.

Session 2 — All about me

Welcome back. In this session you are going to be finding out about *you* and what makes you tick. We are all different and that is why some of us are good at one thing, some of us another, some of us lose our tempers, some of us do not. All of us have to learn to control our tempers so that we do not hurt ourselves or other people. It is OK to feel angry – and we need to learn to put this into words rather than actions. Take a moment to think of something that would make you very angry, and rightly so. What would you feel like doing? What could you do instead?

This would make me **REALLY** angry . . .

_____

_____

It would make me feel I wanted to . . .

_____

_____

But that would be **TERRIBLE** so, instead, I . . .

_____

_____

Talk to me about your family. Write down all the things each member of the family is good at. Which are the same? Which are different? Write down who gets cross quickly. What are the different things you each get cross about, do you think? Here is an example of what the lists might look like.

What we're all good at	
Mum	Shopping for chocolate biscuits, making the dog behave, cooking a good dinner, taking me to school, mending things, fixing the car
Grandad	Watching football with me, cooking curry, telling stories, telling my sister to shut up, giving cuddles when I've hurt myself
Sister	Making a noise, reading, playing monsters with, water fighting
Me	Drawing monsters, making models, collecting dinosaurs, football, playing the drums

Who gets cross in our family?	
Mum gets cross	when I argue with my sister; when Dad shouts at her; when things don't work; when I leave my shoes at the foot of the stairs; when I broke the window
Grandad gets cross	if we make too much noise when he's having a nap; when he's late to go somewhere and we're not ready to get in the car; when the dog makes messes
My sister gets cross	when I go into her room; when I tease her about her hair; when I tell tales on her
I get cross	about not getting things right; if I'm in a bad mood and someone says 'no' to something I want to do; if I'm busy and I'm told to go to bed

Draw a picture for your work box on two sheets of paper. The first should show your head (looking happy) with a huge think bubble at the top. Into this space write down all the things you are good at and feel proud of. I will help. On the next page, draw yourself looking cross and write down in the bubble space all the things you get angry about. There is an example here to look at. It's OK to tell me – it won't worry me because I'm here to help you learn all about temper! We'll talk together about what will be confidential – what are 'good secrets'?

Actually, we all have *two* kinds of brain. We each have a *logical* part of our brain that is good at thinking, remembering, learning things. We also each have an *emotional* part of our brain that is good at feelings and telling our logical brain whether things are safe or not. You probably know that human beings as we know them today developed from cave dwellers thousands of years ago. We had to have these two kinds of brain – you had to know whether to run for it if you saw a beast (and feel worried) or whether to chase the beast and eat it up (and that takes a hot temper) – it is known as 'fight or flight'.

Let's think about that for a moment. When something new or different happens (perhaps a new teacher at school), is your first reaction to feel anxious and worried or to feel cross and 'defensive'? Perhaps it all depends? Let's think about your reactions for a while and write some of them down on a piece of paper for your work box.

When something new and strange happens like . . .
this is how it makes me feel . . .

So far we have learned that we each have an emotional part of our brain and it is important thing to have. Some people never lose their tempers. They never get worked up about anything. They are called 'laid back'. Other people have very short tempers. The trouble is, their emotional brain is shouting too loud for their logical brains to think clearly. Think about times when this has happened to you and talk to me about them. Sadly, when we lose our tempers it can cause problems for us. Let's write down some of the times when you lost your temper. What happened next? Here is an example.

I got really cross when . . .	
	I was busy with my model and Mum said 'go to bed RIGHT NOW'. Last time it happened, I shouted at her and threw my model at her.
	They let my sister do something and then wouldn't let me do what I wanted to do, then I got really cross. Sometimes I wait till later and then look for an excuse to really 'lose it' with her.

Now it's your turn.

I got really cross when . . .

But we now know that we can train our tempers to stay calmer – and that is exactly what you are going to do. So you will end up noticing when your temper is about to go, but then telling it to stop. That's the aim of our work together. Is that OK with you?

Let's gather all the writing we have done this session and put it in your work box. Would you like to file it in the big file or shall we mount it with glue in a scrapbook? You choose.

That's it for today!

Session 3 — My fireworks

OK, so we now know a little more about what makes you tick and what makes you angry.

Losing your temper is a bit like setting off a firework. Think of a firework with a long fuse of blue paper. It won't go off unless someone lights the paper – let's call this a 'trigger'. In the same way, you don't usually lose your temper unless something has happened to lead up to it. Think of some examples.

Once the fuse is lit, then it has to glow for a while as the spark creeps up towards the firework. If you spotted it glowing at this stage, you could still put the firework out with a good bucket of water. But once the spark has reached the firework, then it's too late to do anything. The firework explodes and if anyone is too close, they could get hurt. You might not be able to stop your fireworks exploding, but you can learn to avoid the triggers that set it off or put it out once it has started to glow. Does that make sense to you?

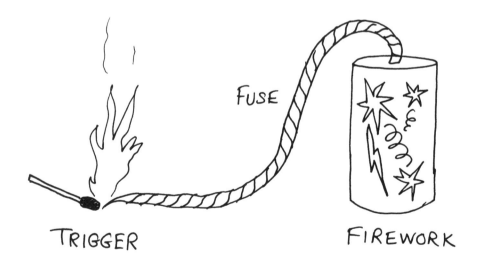

Let's think about your 'triggers' – the things that 'start you off' when your fireworks explode. In your case, think about what your big triggers are – what starts your fuse glowing? Here is an example. Talk it through and decide what makes you angry.

What starts me off . . .	✓/✗	Comments
Being interrupted when I'm busy		
Someone calling me names		
When Dad shouts at me		
When something I'm doing goes wrong		
My brother interfering with my game		
When my sister goes into my bedroom		
My schoolwork going wrong		
When someone knocks into me		
When people won't play with me		
When I get told off and other people don't		
Mum not listening to me		
When Dad tells me what to do		
Losing at football		
Lots of noise when I'm watching TV		
Things getting broken		
When I lose something		

Now decide how *you* are affected. I could do it too, perhaps, so that we are sharing it together.

What starts you off . . .	What starts me off . . .

Session 4 — All about fuses

Hello again. OK, so we now know what gets your fuse lit – the triggers. Let's find out about what happens to you when your fuse starts to glow . . . what does it make you do?

What happens when you worry?

N = Never   S = Sometimes   O = Often   A = Always

	N	S	O	A
1) I can't concentrate				
2) I shout				
3) It frightens me				
4) It makes other people cross				
5) I start to fight				
6) I swear at people				
7) I get headaches				
8) I hit or kick people				
9) I throw things				
10) I throw myself down				
11) I want to run away				
12) My hands go into fists				
13) I start to sweat				

N = Never S = Sometimes O = Often A = Always	N	S	O	A
14) My heart races				
15) I breathe more quickly				
16) I go red				
17) My mouth feels dry				
18) I feel hot and shaky				
19) I start to fidget				
20) I feel tense all over				
Anything else?				

If you have many of these problems, then they are well worth working on, aren't they? This is why we are working hard together to find out more about how your fireworks work. Many of the things that are a problem for you are almost certainly a problem for other people too. Let's work back down the list and think of the effect that each item has on others as well. Even if you feel that going red and clenching your fists affects only you, the fact is that you look angry to other people and this might make others behave differently towards you. It works a bit like a mirror – you get angry and it makes other people angry too.

When I lose my temper, I . . .	This is how it might affect others

Session 5

Spotting a trigger

If you are going to learn how to handle your fireworks, you need to be able to spot those things around you that are likely to cause you anger – we called these 'triggers'. This is important because we are all different. Let's look together at this story about Jake and see if you can spot the triggers, the fuse and the fireworks.

Jake didn't really enjoy school at all. He was happiest when he was outside playing football with his friends. He was good at football and would like to be the team captain and tell everyone else where to play and what to do. Jake lived with his grandma 'Nan' and his dad. On a school morning, he would wake up feeling very grumpy. He would scowl at his nan when she woke him up and take no notice. Soon she would have to shout at him and he would shout back. He was always late for breakfast and would take it out on his nan.

In class, he was quiet and sullen. He did not like it when his teacher told him to do things and he didn't like the work because he didn't find it as easy as playing football. Break-times were good though. The trouble was, he would often get in trouble for playing too wildly and get sent in. That would make him even crosser and he would be rude to teachers. One day, one of the dinner ladies shouted at him and he lashed out at her and bruised her arm. He ran off and hid in the toilets, banging the doors and shouting. That was when the head teacher sent for his dad and he had to go home.

What are the triggers?	Being told to do something he didn't want to; going to school; getting excited during football; doing work.
What did he do when his fuse was glowing?	Get grumpy /go quiet/stop being helpful.
What did he do when his fireworks went off?	Shouted/lashed out.
What could Jake do about it?	Talk about how he feels; ask Nan to talk to the teacher about his difficult work; learn to stay calm at football – join a club perhaps; staying calm and not reacting; letting others be in charge sometimes; develop a plan so he feels more in control.

Now think about the triggers in *your* life. We all have different ways of reacting to anxiety and stress that kick in at different levels. The picture below shows you an example of this for Jake. The length of the fuse is all to do with how many demands are being made on you – that means how many things you are being expected to do – and how awake and ready to go you are. Have you noticed that when you feel really cross about something it makes you more 'aroused' . . . perhaps you start pacing up and down or bite your fingernails, perhaps your heart starts to beat faster and perhaps you breathe faster? Some people at this stage start to feel worried and anxious – others begin to feel cross.

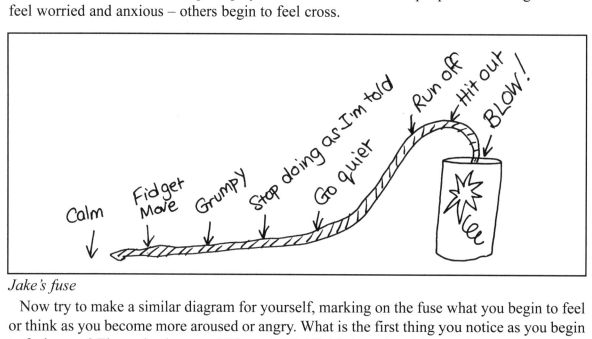

Jake's fuse

Now try to make a similar diagram for yourself, marking on the fuse what you begin to feel or think as you become more aroused or angry. What is the first thing you notice as you begin to feel angry? Then what happens? Then what? All this is to do with your fuse glowing. What you have drawn is a very special diagram and a very useful one. If you can spot what you feel at different stages, you can actually learn ways of making the symptoms go away and this makes you feel less angry – you can control where you are on the fuse so that you are at the right level *for you*.

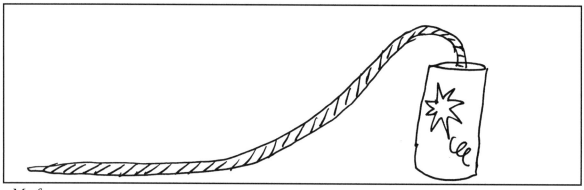

My fuse

Session 6: Acting it out

Last time we did some thinking about triggers that light our anger fuse. Now let's pick out a couple of role plays which would be most helpful for us both to do. Each one is about a child called 'Jo' – you can imagine Jo to be a boy or a girl and whatever age you decide. If you like, you could use puppets or models from your toys to act these situations out. Acting situations out helps you see how things feel from the inside. We will spend a little time role playing these together and for each one we will think about:

- the biggest trigger;
- the effect it has on Jo;
- what would be a bad thing to do;
- what would be a better thing to do;
- plan our advice for Jo.

Role play

Jo is queuing up for lunch at school and gets pushed from behind.
Jo is playing a board game and starts to lose.
Jo's sister gets given a new toy and Jo feels jealous.
Jo's T-shirt gets dirtied by someone else's dinner.
Jo is told to tidy up the sitting room before watching TV.
Jo unwraps a present from Grandma and finds it is the wrong label of jeans.
Jo wants a mobile phone and is not allowed to have one.
Someone calls Jo a liar.
People call Jo names as they walk past.

Invent more to suit you and *your* fireworks.

Session 7 & 8 — Relax!

In these sessions we are going to think about three approaches for calming everything down and stopping yourself feeling tense and angry. However, they each take a bit of practice so you need to choose the one you feel most comfortable with and spend time becoming good at it. Think about all these approaches and choose one to practise over the next few weeks.

1. The balloon method

We need to find a bag of party balloons for this activity.

Let's play with the party balloons, blowing them up and letting a few race uncontrolled around the room as the air escapes rapidly. Now watch me carefully as I start to blow the balloon up and it becomes just that bit too tight. What might happen? (It might burst). What do we need to do? (Let some air out). What would happen if you knocked my hand now? (Try it and see – the balloon whizzes out of control).

Explain that when your fuse starts to glow, it's a little like being a balloon that's just too tight – the slightest knock sets the fireworks off. What do you do when you get knocked? (Lash out/lose my temper/scream at someone).

Let's practise blowing the balloon up and then letting air out gently. When you are feeling tight, you can breathe slowly and gently and your balloon won't feel so tight. Let's practice breathing slowly and gently – slightly longer out than in – breathe as I count: 'IN for one – two – three – four – five . . . OUT for one – two – three – four – five – six – seven'. Keep going and imagine yourself going soft and floppy like a spent balloon.

What you are learning to do is to use *your breathing* to calm down your body.

2. The special place

Another way to stay calm is to close your eyes and think of a calm, relaxing place where it is impossible to feel angry. At first, this is hard. If you practise, you can get to your calm place in your mind quickly and it can actually alter how you feel, changing angry feelings into calm ones.

My Special Place

My special place looks like this

When I am there, this is how I feel

Keep it safe in your work box to look at again. When you start to feel your fuse beginning to glow, try closing your eyes for a moment, take some deep slow breaths and see this special place in your mind's eye. Practise now – think of something that makes you really angry. Hold it for a while – now relax and go to your special place!

You need to practise going in your mind's eye to this special place at least three times through this next week and learn how to do it.

3. Relaxation

Another way of training your body to stay calm is to practise relaxing. If you choose to practise this method, you will need a tape recorder or a recordable CD to make our own relaxation tape. Let's work out together how we will do this – perhaps I could read the script into the recorder as you do the actions so that we get the timing right. We will finish by drawing up a relaxation timetable for you for the next week, writing down when and where you will practise relaxation. For the first three weeks, this should be every day. Then it should be just two or three times a week or when you feel in an angry mood.

Notes for adults

Find a quiet, warm and comfortable place to do your relaxation where you will not be disturbed. For professionals working with children out of home, this can be adjusted to lying back in an armchair with hands placed loosely in the lap rather than having to lie down. Most children also enjoy relaxing music playing quietly in the background as you record your script. Speak slowly and steadily, leaving gaps where you need to – this is why it is helpful for the child to model the actions as you record the text. Slow the whole pace of the actions right down. Do not rush anything.

Just relax!

Lie down flat on your back, close your eyes and take a minute to go as floppy and soft as you can. Imagine you are a big cushion settling down onto the carpet. Let your feet fall gently outward. Let your arms lie by your sides with the hand slightly upwards. Try to breathe slowly and steadily, letting your breath become smoother as it flows in and out like soft waves on the shore.

Now you are feeling floppy and calm. Tighten your feet, pushing the toes backwards towards your head – hold it – and now let go. Let them fall back into place. Feel the difference as you tighten once more – then let go.

Now tighten up your knees so that your legs stick out like sticks. Hold it for a few seconds. Now let go. Can you feel your legs going floppy? Do this once more – tighten – then let go.

Now squeeze your bottom and the tops of your legs together and hold this. As you breathe out, let them relax and become floppy again. Do this once more – squeeze – hold – and relax.

Tighten your tummy and hold it for a few seconds – then relax. Take a few slow breaths. Now tighten, hold, relax and breathe once more.

Spend a few minutes just noticing how floppy and heavy the bottom half of your body has become. Think of each part and check that it feels completely floppy and soft – your toes – your feet – your heels – your calves – your knees – your thighs – your bottom – your tummy.

Clench your fists tightly and feel the difference as you let go and help your hands become floppy again. Try this once more – clench tight – now relax.

Stiffen your elbows so that your arms poke out like sticks. Hold this – and relax again. Notice the difference. One more time – stiffen – hold – relax.

Tighten your shoulders and hunch them up to your neck. Hold them tight and then let them flop. Take a breath. Now tighten once more – hold – relax and breathe. Let the whole of your arms go completely soft.

Close your eyes very tightly and notice how this feels. Let them relax again and try this one more time – squeeze shut – hold – and then relax.

Frown so that your forehead becomes tight – hold it – and now let your face relax and go smooth. Frown once more – hold – and relax. Notice how it feels when your face is smooth and relaxed and there are no frown lines.

Clamp your teeth shut and close your lips tightly. Feel how tight this feels – and now relax. Try this one more time – tight – now loose again.

Lift your head for a moment – feel how heavy it is and let it fall gently back to the floor. Lift once more – hold – and gently back. Turn it to the right until it feels just a little tight – then to the left – and now let it lie back gently into position. Turn to the left, then over to the right – and now back into place.

Now think about your breathing. Feel the air flowing smoothly in – and out – and try to think only of your breaths coming and going like the gentlest of waves. Spend a few minutes staying as relaxed, soft and floppy as you can.

Now it is time to bring your body back into action. Waggle your toes – your legs – your hands – your arms – shrug your body – and gently rock your head – and very soon it is time to get up.

After we have counted, move slowly and carefully as you get up again so that your head gets used to being up in the air again – 5 – 4 – 3 – 2 – 1 and – very slowly – up you get. Well done.

Session 9   Speaking out

> **Notes for adults**
>
> This session is most suitable for children of seven or over. You will have to adapt the words for younger children if you decide to use it. Try using the words 'angry' instead of 'aggressive', 'cool' instead of 'assertive' and 'doing nothing' instead of 'passive'.

Do you remember we talked about how some people begin to feel anxious as they get 'aroused' and others begin to feel angry? This is rather like bottling things up. Sometimes we are not very good about saying what we feel and we may need to do some work on 'being assertive'. Talk to me about what this means. Should you always say what is on your mind? When is it best to 'bottle it up'? For example, if your grandma gave you a present and you didn't like it, would you tell her?

If something is upsetting them, some people speak out - this is being assertive. Some are passive and just let other people 'walk all over them' or just 'switch off'. Others get angry and 'stroppy'. Have you noticed this in people? Try thinking of some examples.

Being assertive means . . .

There are some times when it's best to 'button up' and not be too assertive. For example . . .

Puppet play – being assertive

We'll find some puppets or some of your toys to act out a few situations and show what a difference it makes. Here is an example you could try with two puppets, Gib and Gub.

Take two puppets. Gib snatches Gub's favourite toy.
First, try making Gub say and do nothing – what does Gib do?
Now have Gub kick up an enormous fuss and lash out. What happens then?
Now have Gub say, 'Please don't take my toy. I'm playing with it. When I've finished, you can have a turn'.
You can also try having Gub ask for help from an adult.

Let's talk about each situation.

In this example, Gub had a choice of three ways of behaving. He could either:

1. Do nothing – this is called being *passive*.
2. React angrily – this is called being *aggressive*.
3. Say calmly what he was feeling and stand up for himself – this is called being *assertive*.

Try to think of some more examples of times when you have choices as to how to react. Here are some ideas to start you off. Why not act them out with the puppets?

Example: You have been waiting patiently in a queue. Someone pushes right in front of you.

Passive: just let them and say nothing;

Aggressive: push them out the way again;

Assertive: say, 'Excuse me, I was here first'.

Example: You have made arrangements to play with your best friend who then tells you that he's too busy and he wants to play with someone else.

Passive:

Aggressive:

Assertive:

Example: Someone has taken the last chocolate biscuit from the tin. You say that it wasn't you (and it wasn't) but you are called a liar.

Passive:

Aggressive:

Assertive:

> *Example:*
> **Passive:**
> **Aggressive:**
> **Assertive**:

Here are some ways in which people learn to be more calm and assertive. See if any apply to you:

- Listening carefully to other people and respecting their feelings.
- Not raising your voice in an angry way.
- Telling people how you are feeling.
- Asking nicely and calmly for things.
- Trying to work out how other people are feeling.
- Saying sorry when you know you've done something wrong.
- Not expecting people to tell you how good you are all the time because you know it yourself.

Sometimes people are too aggressive and this gets them into trouble. Does this apply to you ever?

- Shouting at people.
- Demanding things.
- Being rude and swearing at people when you don't get your way.
- Making others feel sad or uncomfortable.
- Hurting other people's feelings.
- Hitting out or kicking other people when they don't agree or want to play.

If we feel that there is an area to work on here, then use this box to help you plan.

> This is what makes me angry . . .

Instead of being aggressive and doing this . . .

I need to be more assertive and do this . . .

However, it won't be easy because this might happen . . .

But I'll try to stay calm by . . .

And when I feel angry I'll talk about it all to this helper . . .

Session 10 — Thinking positively

Notes for adults

This session is most suitable for children of seven or over. Try adapting it for younger children if you think they can manage, or skip it until they are older.

Sometimes it is our *thinking* that gets us into trouble. Because we *think* angry thoughts, we *do* angry actions. Perhaps someone has pushed into you when you are playing outside. You have a choice about how you think about this. You can either think, 'He wants a fight' and start to push and fight him or you can think, 'He tripped' or 'He didn't mean it' or 'He's in a hurry' and just let him pass. *You don't have to react.*

In other words, it is our own angry thoughts that trigger our angry fuses. If you can spot that you tend to think like this, you can actually make yourself see things a new way and stop yourself being so angry. This is another way of lengthening your fuse. Let's think of a few examples.

Example: Mum won't listen when you tell her how you tore your jeans.

Angry thought: She doesn't care.
Angry behaviour: Shouting and running off.
Positive thought: She's worried about it.
Positive behaviour: Say sorry that it's happened and wait till she's calmed down to explain.

Example: Your sister has snatched your bike from you.

Angry thought: She wants a fight.
Angry behaviour: Running after her and dragging her off it.
Positive thought: She really likes my bike. I'm not surprised – it's a good one!
Positive behaviour: (Depending on your situation) Tell Mum/Wait for her to come back and tell her to ask nicely next time/Don't leave it unattended next time.

Example: You are not picked for a team.
Angry thought:
Angry behaviour:
Positive thought:
Positive behaviour:

Example:
Angry thought:
Angry behaviour:
Positive thought:
Positive behaviour:

Talk to your helper about times when you have angry thoughts. Think through times when people have made you really angry and then see whether there might have been another way to think about things. Sometimes, trying to put yourself in someone else's shoes is helpful – if you can work out why *they* appear to be angry or worried themselves, it helps you explain why they are behaving like they are. This can help you not to get angry yourself.

I remember when ....

....

made me really angry because ....

....

I thought ....

....

but perhaps I could have thought ....

....

Anger is a bit like a box of fireworks, isn't it? If one fuse goes off, everyone else's fireworks can get set off too. By making sure your own fuse doesn't get lit, you can stop their fireworks controlling yours. That way, you stay in control of your feelings.

Session 11: Making a plan

You are now ready to think about your own style of dealing with your fireworks and to make plans for changing if you find that this would be helpful. You have thought of a few ways of doing this already. It could mean:

- being more assertive and less aggressive when this seems right;
- spotting the triggers and finding a new way of dealing with them;
- asking for more help when you feel out of control;
- spotting when something has lit your fuse and putting out the spark before it blows the firework;
- thinking more positively about what is happening to you.

Spend this session putting together a plan with your helper. Think through:

- what you will do to stop yourself getting too angry;
- what might get in the way of it working;
- who will help you.

Here is an example of a target sheet completed by Lal – you can imagine Lal to be a boy or a girl and any age.

My target

Start date: 15th February

Target date: End of March

My problem with anger is this: I hate being told what to do and lose my temper if Mum or Dad tell me to do something I don't want to do. This gets me into trouble and everyone gets grumpy. We're all unhappy.

This is what I will do about it: Mum and I will agree a timetable of what I need to do and when. There will be just a few house rules that really matter. Mum will give me reminders and stay calm. She'll give me a count of three to do things. She'll thank me for helping. I'll try to do what she asks – though it might not be straight away if I'm really busy.

This is who will help me and what they will do: Mum is going to put a marble in a jar each time she asks me to do something and I (eventually) do it without shouting at her. I can swap 10 marbles for a treat.

This is what might go wrong and what I'll do: If I'm really busy or feeling grumpy I might flash at her without thinking. So I'll try to stay calm (using the balloon method) and Mum will give me time to 'come round' without shouting or nagging.

My target is: I will do as I am nicely asked three times out of four and Mum won't lose her temper with me.

I will know that it's working because: I'll have lots of marbles in the jar.

This is what will happen if I stick to my target over this time: A family outing to Wonder World during the school holidays!

And now it's your turn to make a plan using the form on the next page.

My target

Start date: Target date:

My problem with anger is this:

This is what I will do about it:

This is who will help me and what they will do:

This is what might go wrong and what I'll do:

My target is:

I will know that it's working because:

This is what will happen if I stick to my target over this time:

Session 12 — How did I do?

Congratulations on all the work you have done on your fireworks course. You now know a lot more about your temper and how it affects you. Doing the course won't act like magic on your temper, but you can now *choose* to use the approaches when you feel angry. Also, you should by now be better able to spot your fuse when it glows so that you know when to find another way of dealing with things.

Practise your approaches as you meet each trigger. If you have been setting targets for your behaviour or the way you deal with other people, then we might look at extending these so you can work for a larger goal and a bigger reward.

You need to know how proud we are that you have worked so hard on this and how pleased we are for you if you are beginning to feel better about things.

This course means that you can now draw up a plan for managing your fireworks so that you can control them more:

- **Spot** when you meet a possible trigger and avoid it.
- **Know** when your fuse is glowing and learn to put it out (for example, what do you first notice? What is it for you?).
- **Tell** yourself what to do (for example, 'Walk away'; 'Be assertive').
- **Take action** – do it! (for example, slow breaths, visit your special place, talk to someone, relax).

Let's think about these questions with your fireworks and your situation in mind.

How I'll cope with my anger

1. **Spot triggers**
   My triggers are . . .

   I can avoid them by . . .

2. **Know when my fuse is glowing**
   I know because . . .

   I can put it out by . . .

3. **Tell myself what to do**
   This is what I'll say . . .

4. **Take action**
   This is what I'll do . . .

And now there's a special certificate for you.
CONGRATULATIONS! Plan a treat to celebrate.

Fireworks Course

_____

has been working hard to control his/her temper
and has now come to the end of the course.

Congratulations!

This is a REAL ACHIEVEMENT

Signed . . . .   Date . . . .

References

Mortimer, H. (2000) *Taking Part: Helping young children take part in a statutory assessment of their special educational needs.* Stafford: QEd Publications.

Mortimer, H. (2007) *Worry Box: Managing anxiety in young children.* Stafford: QEd Publications.

Stockton-on-Tees Educational Psychology Service (2001) *Managing your 4–8 year-old.* Stafford: QEd Publications.

Stockton-on-Tees Educational Psychology Service (2001) *Managing your 8–12 year-old.* Stafford: QEd Publications.

Stockton-on-Tees Educational Psychology Service (2002) *Managing your 13–16 year-old.* Stafford: QEd Publications.

Useful books and resources

Drost, J. (2004) *Bubblegum Guy: How to deal with how you feel.* Bristol: Lucky Duck Publishing (www.luckyduck.co.uk)

Faupel, A., Herrick, E. & Sharp, P. (1998) *Anger Management: A Practical Guide for Teachers, Parents and Carers.* London: David Fulton Publishers.

Hromek, R. (2005) *Game time: Games to Promote Social and Emotional Resilience for School Age Children.* London: Sage Publications (www.sagepub.co.uk)

Koeries, J., Marris, B. & Rae, T. (2004) *Problem Postcards: Social, Emotional and Behavioural Skills Training for Disaffected and Difficult Children aged 7–11.* London: Paul Chapman Publishing (www.paulchapmanpublishing.co.uk)

Mortimer, H. (2003) *Emotional Literacy and Mental Health in the Early Years.* Stafford: QEd Publications (www.qed.uk.com)

Mortimer, H. (2006) *Behaviour Management in the Early Years.* Stafford: QEd Publications (www.qed.uk.com)

Mortimer, H. (2006) *An A-Z of Tricky Behaviours in the Early Years.* Stafford: QEd Publications (www.qed.uk.com)

Mosley, J. (1998) *More Quality Circle Time.* Cambridge: LDA (www.ldalearning.com)

Plummer, D. (2001) *Helping Children to Build Self-Esteem.* London: Jessica Kingsley Publishers (www.jkp.com)

Rae, T. (2001) *Strictly Stress: Effective Stress Management for High School Students.* Bristol: Lucky Duck Publishing (www.luckyduck.co.uk)

Sher, B. (1998) *Self-esteem Games.* Chichester: Wiley (www.wiley.co.uk)

Shotton, G. (2002) *The Feelings Diary.* Bristol: Lucky Duck Publishing (www.luckyduck.co.uk)

Being Yourself – hand puppets and therapeutic games for professionals working to improve mental well-being and emotional literacy in children (www.smallwood.co.uk)

Bridge of Self-Confidence – a therapeutic and educational game for helping coping skills (www.winslow-cat.com)